GOD'S BRILLIANTLY BIG CREATION STORY

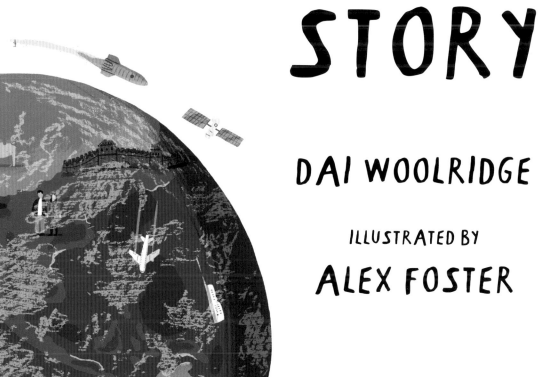

DAI WOOLRIDGE

ILLUSTRATED BY

ALEX FOSTER

D1717105

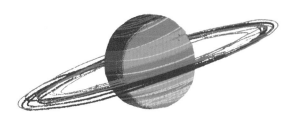
spck

Right at the kick off, God created the cosmos.

God capital G,

made creation capital C.

See, before there was nothing capital N,

but God speaks, snaps his fingers

CLICK

and then?

DID YOU KNOW, THE MILKY WAY IS MADE UP OF
SEVERAL 100 BILLION STARS? (AND THAT'S JUST IN
OUR GALAXY.) IT'S THOUGHT THERE ARE AROUND
100 BILLION GALAXIES, CONTAINING
BILLIONS MORE STARS!

The heaven and earth are birthed
by his words –
a beautifully brilliant burst
of the universe,
God's creation.
Made up of countless
constellations

of several million solar systems
and several billion stars
of planets upon planets like Jupiter and Mars,
'cos in the beginning
the big brilliant boss
made space, made matter, he made the cosmos.

Yet the earth was still . . . **empty**

like a lounge without seats

like a shop without sweets

like a rapper without beats —

we're talking opposite of **plenty** —

BUT . . . not for long.

See, God was in charge and was going to plan it,

with his glory surfing the surface of the planet.

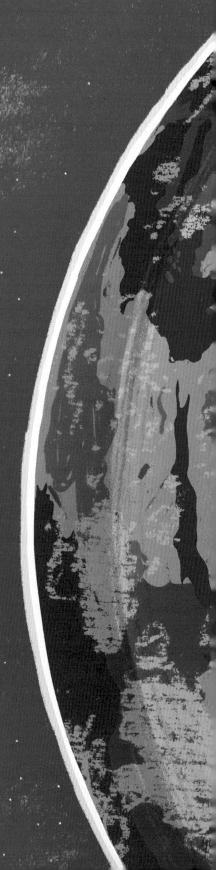

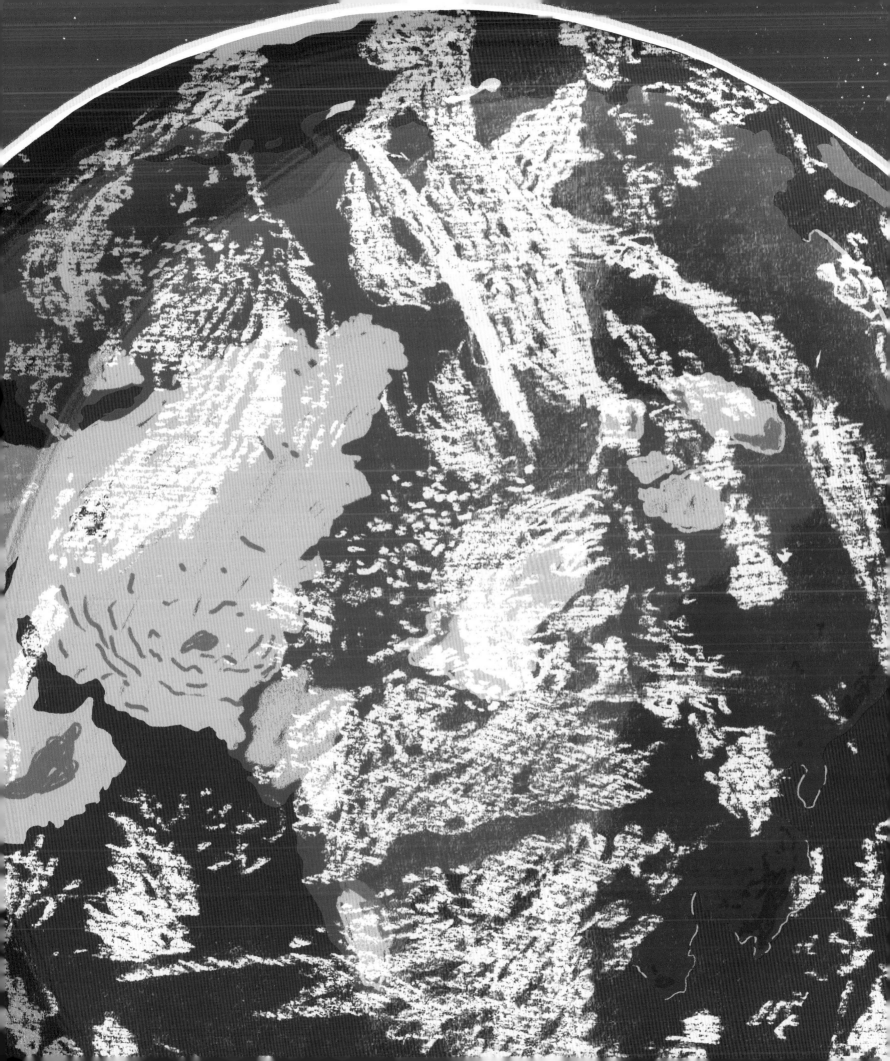

LIGHTNING, AT ITS CORE TEMPERATURE,
IS FIVE TIMES HOTTER THAN THE SURFACE OF THE SUN!
'AND I THOUGHT GRANDAD'S FRESHLY BAKED
SCONES WERE HOT - OUCH!'

'LIGHTS!' God said,

then the light lit up the night

like lightning.

It was a good kind of frightening

as night and day

got a different time frame,

as day became light

and the dark was called night.

Then . . . **'SKY!'**

said God,

and a space was made between sea and the sky.

With God's blue sky thinking

he puts clouds up high,

light fluffy fun ones and grey grumpy glum ones,

he made droplets of rain, and colourful rain-shows

as he illuminated rain into radiant rainbows.

REALLY HIGH

The sea was below, and the rain

poured above it

and God scanned his craftsmanship and said,

'Yeah, I LOVE it!'

Next – **'ROCKS!'**

Let the rocks rock up and make land,

see the ground split the sea exactly as planned.

Caves and cliffs with land that was grand,

AND mega mountains at the peak of their heights

next to vast valleys, what a brilliant sight!

They were made up of mud, and rocks that were rough,

God looked over his handiwork: **'This is GOOD stuff!'**

And then – **'TREES!**
GRASS, FIELDS,' God said,
and just like that the world
spread with VEG!

Tropical-tall-trees and pods-full-of-peas

and freshest-fruit nestled next-to-the-leaves,

appetizing-apples, these aren't simply rumours,

batches of bananas and so-sweet satsumas,

figs on twigs and cherries a-pair,

grapes on vines and pears to share,

all-the-greens, in-the-shops, that-you-see, are-on-sale

God even made superfoods – like spinach and kale!

Even the salads, yes, he made those too!

God checked it all out and said, **'This is SO COOL!'**

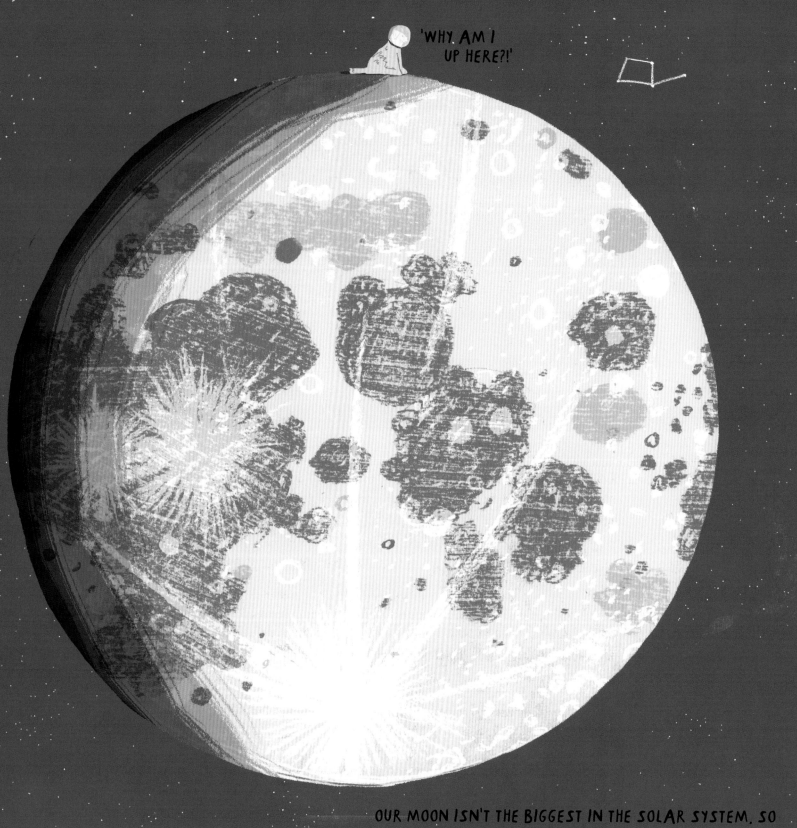

OUR MOON ISN'T THE BIGGEST IN THE SOLAR SYSTEM. SO
FAR, THE BIGGEST MOON WE'VE DISCOVERED IS GANYMEDE,
ONE OF THE 79 MOONS OF JUPITER. 'WHAT - 79 MOONS?!
COME ON JUPITER, THAT'S JUST SHOWING OFF!'

Next, **'SKY LIGHTS!'**

See, God pinned up lights

and he switched on the sun that lit the day bright,

and as he reflected, the maker made room,

in-the-sky he made moon,

a great glow in the night,

sharing the sky with stars that were bright —

near, far and further away . . .

God said of his universe, **'Now that's a display!'**

THE CHALLENGER DEEP IN THE MARIANA TRENCH
IN THE PACIFIC OCEAN IS THE DEEPEST PART OF THE OCEAN
AT MORE THAN 10,000 METRES FROM SEABED TO SURFACE,
THAT'S 95 WHOLE FOOTBALL PITCHES LONG!

And then? God filled the seas!

Oysters and octopus,

mackerel and mussels,

eels and seals

and deep-sea turtles.

See what I mean? It was a sea-filled story

with clownfish like Nemo – you'll even 'find Dory'!

Sharks and squid,

coral and cod,

God took a look,

'This is awesome,' said God.

Then 'BIRDS,' said God,
and suddenly in the sky
were birds of all kinds that could soar,
swoop and fly.

He made pigeons and puffins and pelicans too,
he made kestrels and kites and white cockatoo,
beautiful birds with wings for their flight,
he even made owls awake in the night!
God said, **'Have fun, birds! Nest-up and make chicks'**
and the birds tweeted praise with a melody mix!

Next up – 'ANIMALS!'
Bulls, dogs and brilliant-bull-frogs,
bats, cats and wonderful wombats,
elephants with trunks and
camels with humps,

NORTH
AMERICA

DID YOU KNOW, THERE
ARE RUMOURED TO BE 8.7 MILLION
SPECIES IN THE NATURAL WORLD?
ALTHOUGH CRAZILY ONLY 14 PER CENT
HAVE BEEN FORMALLY IDENTIFIED!

AFRICA

SOUTH
AMERICA

monkeys that swing and
crickets that jump,
koalas up trees,
butterflies that breeze,
things that go BUZZ,
like beautiful bees,

even the bugs, all creepy crawl-ies!
Grasshoppers that hop,
salamanders that slither,
he made crocs and hippos that
hang by the river!

Think of a creature.
That's right, you name it!
God said the word,
just like that – he made it!

EUROPE

ASIA

AUSTRALIA & OCEANA

ANTARCTICA

It was all good –
BUT God raised the bar
by far.

He made the greatest of creatures, with
Godlike features,

you should've seen him at work,
you'd be totally speechless!

He moulded magnificently,

formed them so wonderfully,
delicately, dextrously and ever so expressively!

He made them . . .
Who? You and me!

Boys and girls, just like
he planned it.
'Look what I've made,'
as God points to the planet,

'from little to large,
this is your crib,
I'm putting you in charge
of it all . . .
the creepers that crawl,
the birds that sing, the fish that swim,
every-thing!'

God took it all in,

   every bit looked good to him.

      It was . . . a masterpiece

         and the master took in every piece.

        And just before he sat back in his seat

     and he kicked off his shoes and he put up his feet,

God saw us and smiled and he said, **'What a feat.**

This is SOO good

     NOW it's complete.'

For our mini Wooly

Thank you to . . .

Cath my best friend, my mischief maker and heart on legs – your love, passion, creativity and support are my fuel that keep me telling the story

Mam you are my joint biggest fan and I am so thankful for you – you have displayed Jesus to me throughout my life

Bob you are a dear friend who inspires me and prods me to keep playing when I pick up the pen

my **Wooly Trotter Evans family, Lounge Church and friends at SOW**

Bible Society for helping me to realize how much I love writing for children

Alex for the AMAZING illustrations, Juliet and all at SPCK.

———————

First published in Great Britain in 2021

Society for Promoting Christian Knowledge
36 Causton Street
London SW1P 4ST
www.spck.org.uk

Text copyright © Dai Woolridge 2021
Illustrations copyright © Alex Foster 2021

All rights reserved. No part of this book may be reproduced or transmitted in any form or by any means, electronic or mechanical, including photocopying, recording, or by any information storage and retrieval system, without permission in writing from the publisher.

British Library Cataloguing-in-Publication Data
A catalogue record for this book is available from the British Library

ISBN 978–0–281–08481–4

1 3 5 7 9 10 8 6 4 2

Printed by Imago

Subsequently digitally printed in Great Britain

Produced on paper from sustainable forests